Reading Together

Incy Wincy Spider
And Other Action Rhymes

Read it together

Incy Wincy Spider brings together a collection of favourite nursery rhymes in which actions are part of the fun.

The pictures give suggestions for actions to accompany each rhyme. Show your child how to use these actions with the rhymes – or use actions you already know.

Talking together about the rhymes and pictures helps your child to make sense of the book.

Encourage your child to join in with you whenever you can. A good way to do this is to let them finish the rhyme.

Out of the hive, One, two ...

three, four, five!

Many of the rhymes in this book will quickly become familiar and this will help your child to say them almost word for word.

Show me the ones you like best.

Jelly on a plate and Row, row, row your boat!

Dickory dickory dock ...

Hickory dickory dock!

You can talk to your child about their favourite rhymes in the book. They might have particular reasons for liking some more than others.

We hope you enjoy reading this book together.

For Charlotte Quarme

First published 1998 by Walker Books Ltd
87 Vauxhall Walk, London SE11 5HJ

This edition published 2005

2 4 6 8 10 9 7 5 3

Candles from TWIDDLING YOUR THUMBS
by Wendy Cope reproduced by kind permission of Faber and Faber Ltd
Illustrations © 1998 Patrice Aggs
Introductory and concluding notes © 1998 CLPE/LB Southwark

Printed in China

ISBN 1-4063-0059-4

www.walkerbooks.co.uk

Incy Wincy Spider
And Other Action Rhymes

Illustrated by **Patrice Aggs**

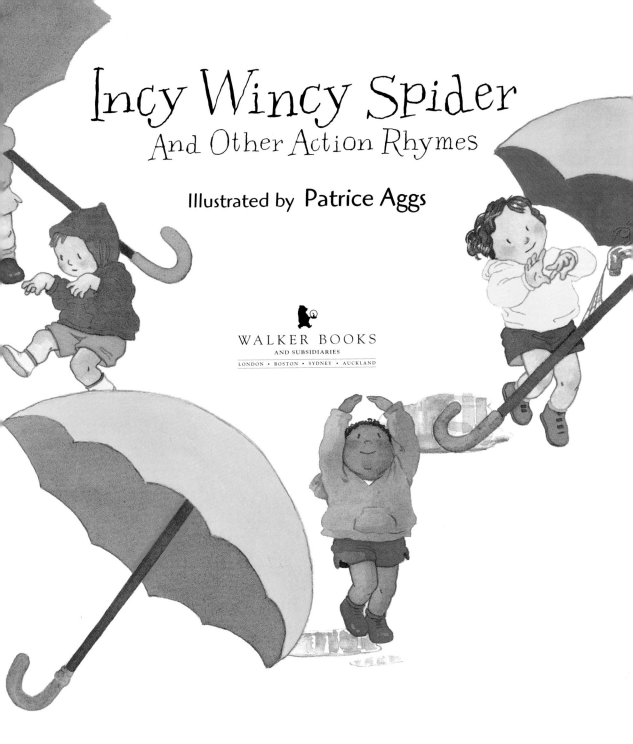

WALKER BOOKS
AND SUBSIDIARIES

LONDON · BOSTON · SYDNEY · AUCKLAND

Pat-a-cake

Pat-a-cake, pat-a-cake, baker's man,
Bake me a cake as fast as you can.
Pat it and prick it and mark it with B,
And put it in the oven for Baby and me.

Five currant buns

Five currant buns in a baker's shop,
Round and fat with a cherry on the top.
Along came a boy with a penny one day,
He bought a currant bun,
And he took it away.

Four currant buns, etc.

Mix a pancake

Mix a pancake
Stir a pancake,
Pop it in the pan.
Fry the pancake
Toss the pancake,
Catch it if you can!

I'm a little teapot

I'm a little teapot, short and stout,
Here's my handle, here's my spout.
When I see the teacups, hear me shout:
Tip me up and pour me out!

Jelly on a plate

Jelly on a plate,
Jelly on a plate,
Wibble wobble,
Wibble wobble,
Jelly on a plate.

Candles

Five little candles
On a birthday cake.
Count them very carefully
So there's no mistake.
We counted five and there's no doubt –
Now it's time to blow them out.

Wendy Cope

The bear went over the mountain

The bear went over the mountain
The bear went over the mountain
The bear went over the mountain
To see what he could see.

But all that he could see
But all that he could see
Was the other side of the mountain
The other side of the mountain
The other side of the mountain
Was all that he could see.

This little piggy

This little piggy
went to market,

This little piggy
stayed at home,

This little piggy
had roast beef,

This little piggy
had none.

This little piggy
went wee, wee, wee,

All the way home!

There was a little turtle

There was a little turtle,
He lived in a box.
He swam in a puddle,
He climbed on the rocks.

He snapped at a mosquito,
He snapped at a flea.
He snapped at a minnow,
He snapped at me.

He caught the mosquito,
He caught the flea.
He caught the minnow,
But he didn't catch me!

Here is the beehive

Here is the beehive,
Where are the bees?
Hidden away
Where nobody sees.

Soon they come creeping
Out of the hive,
One, two, three, four, five!

One, two, three!

One, two, three!
Mother catch a flea,
Flea die, mother cry,
One, two, three!

Mosquito one

Mosquito one,
Mosquito two,
Mosquito jump in
De ole man shoe;

De ole man cry,
De ole man cry,
De ole man cry
Like a little chile.

Hickory dickory dock

Hickory dickory dock,
The mouse ran up the clock.
The clock struck one,
The mouse ran down,
Hickory dickory dock.

A mouse lived in a little hole

A mouse lived in a little hole,
Lived softly in a little hole,
When all was quiet as quiet can be ...
OUT POPPED HE!

Row, row, row your boat

Row, row, row your boat
Gently down the stream,
Merrily, merrily, merrily, merrily,
Life is but a dream.

Row, row, row your boat
Gently down the stream,
If you see a crocodile,
Don't forget to scream!

One, two, three, four, five

One, two,
three, four, five,

Once I caught
a fish alive.

Six, seven,
eight, nine, ten,
Then I let him go again.

Why did you
let him go?

Because he bit
my finger so.

Which finger did he
bite? This little finger
on the right.

I hear thunder

I hear thunder,
I hear thunder.
So do I,
So do I.
Pitter-patter raindrops,
Pitter-patter raindrops.
I'm all dry,
So am I.

I hear thunder,
I hear thunder.
Hark, don't you?
Hark, don't you?
Pitter-patter raindrops,
Pitter-patter raindrops.
I'm wet through,
So are you!

Incy Wincy Spider

Incy Wincy Spider
Climbed the water spout.
Down came the rain
And washed poor Incy out.
Out came the sun
And dried up all the rain,
Incy Wincy Spider
Climbed up the spout again.

Oh, the grand old Duke of York

Oh, the grand old Duke of York,
He had ten thousand men,
He marched them up to the top of the hill,
And he marched them down again.

And when they were up, they were up,
And when they were down, they were down,
And when they were only half way up,
They were neither up nor down.

Oh, my grand old Grandpa York

Oh, my grand old Grandpa York,
He had ten thousand teds,
He marched them into their baths every night,
Then he marched them to their beds.

And when they got in, they were wet,
And when they got out, they were dry,
And when they were all snuggled up very tight,
He sang them a lullaby.

Clap your hands, stamp your feet

If you're happy and you know it,
Clap your hands;
If you're happy and you know it,
Clap your hands;
If you're happy and you know it
And you really want to show it,
If you're happy and you know it,
Clap your hands!

If you're happy and you know it,
Stamp your feet, etc.
If you're happy and you know it,
Nod your head, etc.
If you're happy and you know it,
Wave your hands, etc.
If you're happy and you know it,
Shout "We are!" etc.

Head, shoulders, knees and toes

Head, shoulders, knees and toes,
Knees and toes,
Head, shoulders, knees and toes,
Knees and toes,
And eyes and ears and mouth and nose,
Head, shoulders, knees and toes,
Knees and toes.

Ring-a-ring o' roses

Ring-a-ring o' roses,
A pocket full of posies.
A-tishoo, a-tishoo!
We all fall down.

Two little dicky-birds

Two little dicky-birds,
Sitting on a wall,
One named Peter,
One named Paul.

Fly away, Peter!
Fly away, Paul!

Round and round the garden

Round and round the garden,
Like a teddy bear,
One step, two step,
Tickle you under there!

Come back, Peter!   Come back, Paul!

Five little ducks went swimming one day

Five little ducks went swimming one day,
Across the lake and far away,
Mother Duck said, "Quack, quack, quack, quack,"
But only four little ducks came back.

Four little ducks went swimming one day,
Across the lake and far away,
Mother Duck said, "Quack, quack, quack, quack,"
But only three little ducks came back.

Three little ducks went swimming one day,
Across the lake and far away,
Mother Duck said, "Quack, quack, quack, quack,"
But only two little ducks came back.

Two little ducks went swimming one day,
Across the lake and far away,
Mother Duck said, "Quack, quack, quack, quack,"
But only one little duck came back.

One little duck went swimming one day,
Across the lake and far away,
Mother Duck said, "Quack, quack, quack, quack,"
And all the five little ducks came back.

Read it again

Row, row ...

row your boat ...

Act it out
This collection of rhymes has suggestions for actions on each page. Doing the actions helps bring the rhymes to life and makes it easier for children to remember them. As you read the rhymes, your child can use the pictures as a guide to the hand or body movements and join in.

I know *Incy Wincy Spider*.

Good – you show me.

Remembering the rhyme
When children hear the rhymes read aloud again and again they will begin to remember them by heart. You can encourage them to tell or act out the ones they know.

Drawing
Your child can draw a picture of a favourite rhyme and tell you the words to go with it. They could make a collection for their bedroom wall.

Using props

To take the action a step further, you can make props together that would be useful for acting out the different rhymes, such as cardboard binoculars for *The bear went over the mountain* or currant buns made of playdough for *Five currant buns*.

The bear went over the mountain ...

To see what he could see.

More action rhymes

There may be other rhymes you know where actions help to make them more fun. You can share these with your child and invent actions together.

Puff, puff, Peep, peep, Off we go!

I'm a little teapot
short and stout
Here's my handle
here's my spout

There was a little turtle, He lived in a box.